NATIONAL GEOGRAPHIC KiDS

BOOK OF PLANETS

CATHERINE D. HUGHES

ILLUSTRATED BY
DAVID A. AGUILAR

NATIONAL GEOGRAPHIC
WASHINGTON, D.C.

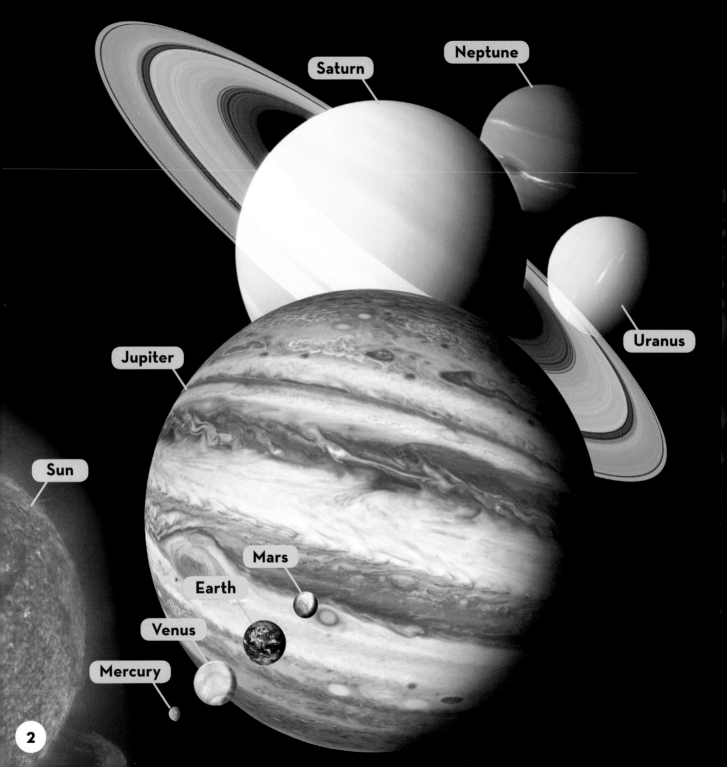

Neptune

Saturn

Uranus

Jupiter

Sun

Mars

Earth

Venus

Mercury

ROCKY PLANETS AND GAS GIANTS

To be called a planet, an object has to be round, and it must orbit a star. Nothing else has its exact same orbit. There are eight big planets that orbit the sun.

The four planets closest to the sun are made mostly of rock. They are called terrestrial, or rocky, planets.

The four planets farthest from the sun are big balls of gas. They do not have a solid surface.

Some things are **SOLID**, like a **ROCK**.

Other things are **GAS**, like the **AIR** you breathe.

And some things are **LIQUID**, like **WATER**.

Can you say the names of all eight big planets on page 2?

Mercury **DOES NOT HAVE** a moon.

MERCURY is hard to see from **EARTH** because it is so close to the bright **SUN.**

MERCURY

Mercury is the planet closest to the sun. It is the smallest of the eight big planets.

It orbits the sun faster than any other planet. One year on Earth, the time it takes to orbit the sun, is 365 days. One year on Mercury is only 88 days.

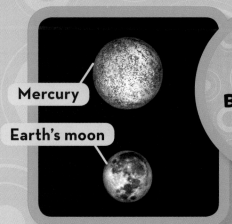

Mercury

Earth's moon

MERCURY is only a **LITTLE BIGGER** than **EARTH'S MOON.**

During the day on Mercury, it gets very hot. At night, it gets very cold.

MERCURY and **VENUS** are the only big planets in our solar system that **DO NOT HAVE MOONS.**

VENUS is the planet **CLOSEST TO EARTH.**

VENUS

Venus is the hottest planet in our solar system. It has an atmosphere of thick clouds. The clouds hold in heat like a blanket, making Venus very hot.

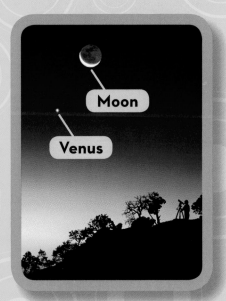

Moon

Venus

The sun's light reflects off Venus's clouds. That makes Venus look very bright. Only the moon is brighter in Earth's night sky.

Can you find Venus in the sky?
HINT: It looks like the brightest star in the sky. But it is a planet, not a star.

Most of **EARTH** is covered by **OCEANS.** The blue areas are water.

Moon

Earth

EARTH is the **FIFTH LARGEST PLANET** in the solar system.

EARTH

A planet is a big, round object in space that orbits a star. Earth is your home. The sun is your star.

Earth is always moving. As it orbits the sun, it also spins around like a top.

EARTH is the **THIRD** planet in orbit around the **SUN.**

EARTH spins at **1,000 MILES AN HOUR.**

When you spin around on your feet you probably get dizzy. But you cannot feel Earth spin.

During the day it is light outside, and you can see the sun.

As Earth spins, the place where you are on the planet turns away from the sun. That is when it gets dark outside.

As Earth keeps spinning, you soon see the sun again. It takes Earth one day and one night—24 hours—to spin all the way around.

When it is **SUMMER** where you live, your part of Earth **IS TILTED TOWARD THE SUN.**

When it is **WINTER** where you live, your part of Earth **IS TILTED AWAY FROM THE SUN.**

The huge **VOLCANOES** on Mars may be **the BIGGEST** in the **SOLAR SYSTEM.**

Deimos

One day on Mars is about the **SAME LENGTH OF TIME** as one day on Earth.

Phobos

MARS

Mars is more like Earth than any other planet in the solar system.

Scientists think there may have been flowing rivers on Mars long ago. They are curious about where the river water is now. It may be frozen beneath the surface.

Mars looks reddish because there is a lot of **IRON** in the **ROCKS** on its surface. **IRON** is a **METAL THAT RUSTS,** turning red.

Several spaceships have traveled to Mars carrying equipment to explore the planet. Robots called rovers roll across the surface taking photographs, looking for water, and studying rocks.

The rover **SOJOURNER** was the **FIRST VEHICLE** with **WHEELS** used to **EXPLORE** another planet.

Sojourner

The rover **SPIRIT** took this photograph of the **SURFACE OF MARS.**

Victoria crater

Two rovers called Spirit and Opportunity landed on two sides of Mars in January 2004. Spirit stopped working in 2010. But Opportunity kept going, continuing to send information back to Earth.

Did Spirit and Opportunity land on Mars before or after you were born?

Curiosity

A rover called **CURIOSITY** was **LAUNCHED** from **EARTH** in 2011 to land on Mars in 2012. One of its jobs: **PICK UP** and look at **ROCKS** on **MARS.**

JUPITER looks striped because it spins very fast, pulling its **CLOUDY ATMOSPHERE** into **BANDS AROUND THE PLANET.**

The **GREAT RED SPOT** is wider than three Earths.

JUPITER

Jupiter is our solar system's biggest planet. It is so big that all the other planets in the solar system could fit inside it.

It takes almost **12 EARTH YEARS** for **JUPITER** to completely **ORBIT THE SUN.**

The huge storm on Jupiter is called the Great Red Spot. The storm is like a hurricane on Earth, but Jupiter's storm has been blowing for hundreds of years!

What kinds of storms do you have where you live?

SATURN has thousands of rings.

SATURN

Look at the sparkly rings around Saturn! Saturn's rings are the biggest and brightest in our solar system.

The rings are made up of billions of bits of icy rocks. Some bits are as tiny as specks of dust. Others are the size of huge mountains.

FACTS

SIZE

Earth

Saturn

SAY MY NAME
SAH-tern

PLACE IN SPACE
Sixth planet in orbit around the sun

HOW FAR AWAY
It takes four years for a spaceship to get there.

SUNLIGHT REFLECTS OFF THE ICE in Saturn's rings and makes them **SPARKLE.**

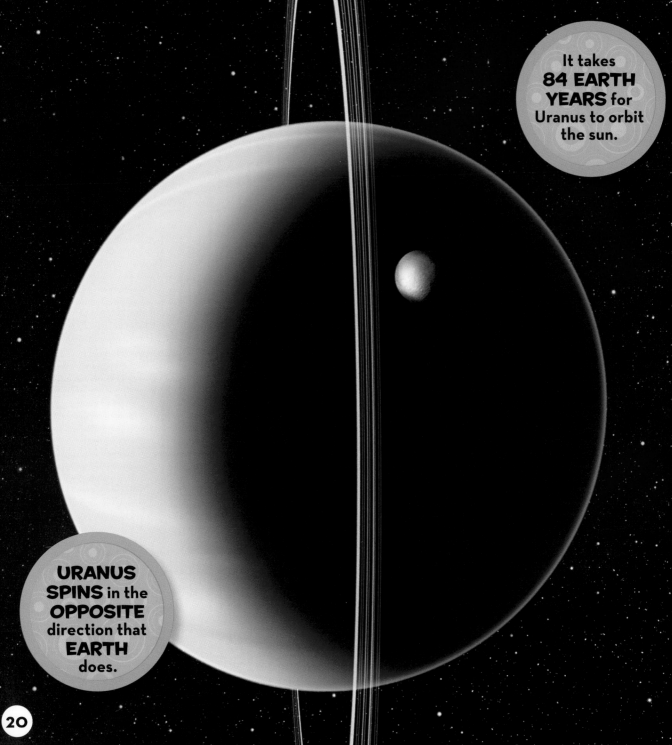

It takes **84 EARTH YEARS** for Uranus to orbit the sun.

URANUS SPINS in the **OPPOSITE** direction that **EARTH** does.

URANUS

Uranus is tipped onto its side. Scientists think that a long time ago some huge space object, the size of a planet, may have crashed into Uranus. That crash caused Uranus to tip.

Compare the pictures of Saturn and Uranus, below. Do you see how Uranus looks tipped?

Saturn

Uranus

Like Jupiter, **NEPTUNE** is known as a **GAS GIANT.**

Great Dark Spot

22

NEPTUNE

Neptune is farther from the sun than any of the other big planets.

The weather on this planet is wild. Winds blow more than a thousand miles an hour!

It takes Neptune **165 YEARS TO TRAVEL** all the way **AROUND THE SUN.**

Remember the Great Red Spot on Jupiter? Neptune also had a big storm like that. On Neptune, it was called the Great Dark Spot. Neptune has many storms that come and go.

FACTS

SIZE

Earth

Neptune

SAY MY NAME
NEP-tune

PLACE IN SPACE
Eighth planet in orbit around the sun

HOW FAR AWAY
It takes 12 years for a spaceship to get there.

GLOSSARY

ASTEROID
a small, rocky space object

ASTEROID BELT
the area between Mars and Jupiter where most asteroids are found in orbit around the sun

ASTRONAUT
a person who travels into space

ASTRONOMER
a person who studies space

ATMOSPHERE
air surrounding a planet

CALLISTO
(kah-LIS-toe) one of the four largest moons orbiting Jupiter

COMET
a space object with a large orbit around the sun, made up of icy gases, rock, and dust

DEIMOS
(DIE-mas) one of two moons orbiting Mars

EUROPA
(yoo-RO-pah) one of the four largest moons orbiting Jupiter

FLYBY
the flight of a spacecraft that passes by a planet, moon, or other space object

GALAXY
a very large group of stars, gas, and dust held together by gravity

GANYMEDE
(GAN-uh-meed) one of the four largest moons orbiting Jupiter

GRAVITY
the strong, invisible force that, for example, keeps things from floating off Earth into the sky

GREAT DARK SPOT
a huge storm on Neptune detected by Voyager 2 in 1989, which was no longer evident in Hubble photographs taken in 1994

GREAT RED SPOT
a huge storm on Jupiter

IO
(EYE-oh) one of the four largest moons orbiting Jupiter

LANDER
a spacecraft that lands on the surface of a planet, moon, or other space object

METEOR
chunk of space rock that burns as it travels through Earth's atmosphere; sometimes called a shooting star

METEORITE
chunk of space rock (meteor) that reaches Earth's surface

MOON
a natural object that orbits a planet

NASA
National Aeronautics and Space Administration, the space program for the United States

NEREID
(NEER-ee-id) third largest moon orbiting Neptune

ORBIT
the path through space around a planet or star

ORBITER
a spacecraft that stays in orbit around a planet, moon, or other object in space without landing

PHOBOS
(FO-bis) one of two moons orbiting Mars

PLANET
a large, round object that orbits a star

PROTEUS
(PRO-tee-us) second largest moon orbiting Neptune

ROCKET
a powerful spacecraft that lifts astronauts and satellites and other equipment into space

SATELLITE
a spacecraft that orbits a planet and is filled with equipment to do jobs such as tracking weather and making maps

SHOOTING STAR
a nickname for a meteor as it burns in Earth's atmosphere

SOLAR SYSTEM
a star and the objects that orbit it

STAR
a bright, shining ball of gases such as Earth's sun, usually seen in the night sky

SUN
the star that is the center of Earth's solar system

SUNGRAZER
a comet that crashes into the sun

SUNRISE
the time when the sun appears in the sky in the morning

SUNSET
the time when the sun disappears from sight in the sky in the evening

TELESCOPE
a piece of equipment, usually shaped like a tube, that makes faraway things look closer

TRITON
(TRI-ton) largest moon orbiting Neptune

UNIVERSE
everything in space